The Law Of Vision

Daniel F. Johnson

ISBN:

DEDICATION

I dedicate this book to my dad and mom and to all my siblings

CONTENTS

ACKNOWLEDGMENTS

Thanks to God almighty for His grace and mercy in my life. I thank everyone that have made massively contributions to me in one way or the other especially my family.

OPENING TEXT AND EXPLANATION

Jeremiah 1:11-12 (KJV) Moreover the word of the LORD came unto me, saying, Jeremiah, what seest thou? And I said, I see a rod of an almond tree.

Then said the LORD unto me, Thou hast well seen: for I will hasten my word to perform it.

Wow! So there Is a relationship between speed and vision. The moment you see well you compare speed in your life because you have seen correctly. I was going to perform it anyway but on the strength and clarity of your vision i will hasten my word to perform it.

Genesis 13:14-15 And the LORD said unto Abram, after that Lot was separated from him, Lift up now thine eyes, and look from the place where thou art northward, and southward, and eastward, and westward:

For all the land which thou seest, to thee will I give it, and to thy seed for ever.

Not the land that is available the one you see is what is given to you. There's verse land available but as far as you can capture that is what will be delivered to you.

WHAT IS VISION?

Vision is a clear picture of the next level of your life, a clear picture of your destiny.

The capacity for or state of seeing.

A person's capacity for imaginative or wise future planning.

A perception of someone or something appearing in a dream, trance, or as a ghostly apparition.

You may visualize the future and utilize

that image to guide your actions when you employ vision. A sense of purpose can be given by using vision as a guide.

This is very powerful, there are many well meaning believers, born again filled with the holy spirit and they have ignore the power of vision to the detriment of their progress. Vision is powerful.

It is in this area that both science and religion agree's that without vision there is no movement. Motion is a function of vision there is no car that does not have a provision to look at, there's no plane that doesn't have a space for sight no matter how manage they must give space for the driver to see because sight is what controls movement.

The pilot must see, the driver must see, the captain must see.

I don't know any creature that has its eyes backwards every creature i know has its eyes forward because you only move in the direction of your eyes.

You can only make giant strive in the spirit when you have a vision, a clear

vision. Now as powerful as vision is it does not profit you remaining as vision, you must break your vision in to goals and break your vision into daily tasks

Untill your vision becomes daily tasks otherwise it will only remain a dream in the realm of the spirit.

There are people who have done well in terms of writing a theme that seems to coordinate their lives but are unable to break the vision in to goals.

WHAT IS A GOAL?

A goal is a desire end, an expected end, a subsets of that vision. There is an energy, there is a power that vision gives when you break your vision into daily tasks it's gives you focus.

Vision gives you the legitimate grounds to say no to so many things. There are many things you will not be able to have the power to say no to untill you have vision.

TIME AND FOCUS

If you are not a man of vision or a woman of vision you may not have the courage to say no to many things. Time will never be enough to mix your vision alongside many distractions you will have to cut away so many things in other to have focus.

The unit of destiny is time whatever you give your time to you are giving part of your life to and you must be sure that every minute and every seconds you commit to anything is what that while.

I do not know any leader who is not

visionary even the devil is visionary. He has is own vision which is to steal, to kill and to destroy no wonder he seems to be succeeding.

Could it be that you are where you are right now because you are hoping God will find away of lifting you, it look spiritual but very wrong. Some of those superstitious believe be delivered from it now in the name of jesus...

TAKE RESPONSIBILITY AND TAKE ACTION

We have many sociological saying they look spiritual because they have been handed down by well intention people but all this things give access to the devil to blend our minds and our progress.

Having the believe that one day my life will be better, without vision? No sir. I know my God He is too faithful to just leave me like that, you are right but with respect to this truth you are wrong.

Hoping that your life will change just

because He is alive or hoping that one day something will just happen is a joke. You must wake up to the vision of your life God does not empower ignorant people.

One day I will have a global Ministry, one day in the name of jesus I will bless people that's wonderful congratulations except for the fact that you are working inline with your vision that's the only way you can achieve your desire result not just sitting somewhere having a random wish from day to day.

THE DIFFERENCE BETWEEN A WISH AND A GOAL

A wish is a desire with no responsibility committed to it. When you set a goal, it is a strong desire that is backed up with the willingness to commit whatever it takes under God to actualize that goal, responsibility is the keyword.

If all you have is just a desire, it will never come to pass. Your desire must be able to sponsor the willingness to pay whatever price under God to see that it come to pass. Are we together?

I am amazed at how many Christians

respectfully speaking live absolutely visionless lives. Some people just move up and down and blame God for everything when they can't see God they blame their pastor who they can see for everything, they blame parents.

I understand that some situations can be very overwhelming understand the fact but the day you start moving forward is the day you take responsibility over your destiny and say in the name of jesus am tired of giving excuses, in the name of jesus am tired of legitimizing the continuity of mediocrity and weakness in my life.

I respect and I sympathize with your background, I sympathize that you came from a family that was not very visionary I sympathize with you but wake up. From where thou art lift up your eyes. For as long you keep looking down you will soon find your children looking with you, you will soon find your grandchildren joining them to look with you.

Many of our parents respectfully speaking kept complaining until will now

join them in that complain you must make up your mind that my children will not find me there in the name of jesus christ.

You are the one God have commissioned to break every circle of poverty, lack and want but it only comes with the power of vision. The reason why God stop showing some people certain things is because He trace that they don't take is speakings serious.

Abraham come out from your father's house, the transformation started when he changed what he was seeing. Hear me you may be in that old apartment now, there is no point faking what can be real just be patient with your destiny.

You see the powerful thing about vision is that it has the power of omini presence, you can be in a room and your vision can be where you will be tomorrow. Imagination is powerful your vision works with your imagination and it can go to your future and make sure it supervises that your future is real it will come back and take your body there.

Vision is powerful...

THE POWER OF VISION

Proverbs 29:18 Where there is no vision, the people perish: but he that keepeth the law, happy is he.

Vision is so powerful that without it your life has no coordination of growth and success.

There is timing to your life and your destiny. Sometimes we over pamper people, we over pamper our children instead of opening them early to the responsibility dimension of life. We keep saying he is a child why they keep behaving strange and it becomes a habit.

AVOID DISTRACTIONS

Friends can call you and say what are you doing this weekend? If you are free why don't you come around tell them am grateful but I have a few books I must finish and these books are connected with what God is doing in my life this season I appreciate you maybe another time.

And you don't feel guilty for it because you are making that sacrifice in honor of where you are going.
Don't let anybody just put you in their

plans without first checking your day plan.

DEFINE YOUR RELATIONSHIPS

Vision defines your relationships, when you know where you are going it will defines who goes with you. If you do not have vision, you will not be able to edit the relationship that comes to your life.

Anybody should not be in your life in the journey of your destiny, just because they are good doesn't mean they are for you. Don't give people the legitimate ground to occupy your life for nothing just because they are good people.

Your vision is the big picture of where you are going. Vision leads to goals, goals leads to daily tasks. When you fulfill your daily tasks, you will fulfill your short term goals that will eventually lead you to fulfilling your vision. Don't just wake up without planning your day. It is better to plan and fail than to not plan.

Make up your mind to be visionary let there be something that your life is all about. Open up your self to a system of mentorship and learning.

When God defines your destiny, the devil will bring people who are not related to your destiny and if you keep moving around such people you will not grow. There have to be something your life is about.

Is everybody around your life going where you are going?

Time is going, opportunity is going what is the vision for your life?

www.ingramcontent.com/pod-product-compliance
Lightning Source LLC
LaVergne TN
LVHW020542160826
845677LV00015B/4160

* 9 7 9 8 3 5 9 6 9 1 0 6 2 *